SAINT FRANCIS

For Arlene,

May the life of Francis,
inspire your life, as he walks
with you on your journey,
as a friend and brother;

John August Swanson

January 15, 2017

SAINT FRANCIS

TEXT BY
MARIE DENNIS

ART BY
JOHN AUGUST SWANSON

Founded in 1970, Orbis Books endeavors to publish works that enlighten the mind, nourish the spirit, and challenge the conscience. The publishing arm of the Maryknoll Fathers and Brothers, Orbis seeks to explore the global dimensions of the Christian faith and mission, to invite dialogue with diverse cultures and religious traditions, and to serve the cause of reconciliation and peace. The books published reflect the views of their authors and do not represent the official position of the Maryknoll Society. To learn more about Maryknoll and Orbis Books, please visit our website at www.maryknoll.org.

Queries regarding rights and permissions should be addressed to:
Orbis Books, P. O. Box 308, Maryknoll, New York 10545-0308.
Queries regarding the art should be directed to:
John August Swanson, 2903 Waverly Drive, Los Angeles, California 90039.

Published by Orbis Books, Maryknoll, NY 10545-0308
Manufactured in the United States of America
Design: Roberta Savage

Library of Congress Cataloging-in-Publication Data

Dennis, Marie.
    Saint Francis/text by Marie Dennis; art by John August Swanson.
        p. cm.
    ISBN 1-57075-412-8
    1. Francis, of Assisi, Saint, 1182–1226—Meditations. I. Swanson,
John August. II. Title.
    BX4700.F6 D44 2002
    271'.302—dc21
                                2001007766

Dedication

This book is dedicated to those among us, who, like Saint Francis of Assisi, transcend limitations and offer extraordinary service to the world in which we live. They are the people who are the peacemakers and the defenders of human rights, empowering others to work for justice. Facing great obstacles and challenges of violence as they work for change, they live out the model of love, courage, and determination found in Saint Francis. We are inspired and made hopeful by their heroic lives as they overcome their fear and weakness.

Contents

Introduction
Marie Dennis

These few words on the life of St. Francis of Assisi are not intended to tell the whole story–volume upon volume have already done so–but to invite the reader to encounter a holy man whose life is still relevant to our own journeys, even after eight hundred years.

John August Swanson's painting of Francis of Assisi is an evocative, brilliant portrayal of Francis' life. His depictions of Francis form a powerful story by themselves. I invite the reader to sit with each picture for a while, and only then, perhaps, to read the accompanying vignette from the life of Francis that is suggested by the artist's visual expression. Most of the vignettes are taken from the writing of Thomas of Celano, Francis' earliest biographer, whose work drew upon many sources, including the testimony of Francis' companions and friends: Brother Leo, Brother Rufino, Brother Angelo, Pope Gregory IX, Bishop Guido, and Saint Clare. A few pictures are more clearly based upon some of the many legends associated with Francis. For these I have included passages from *The Little Flowers of St. Francis*, translated by Raphael Brown, a collection of some of the best-loved stories about the saint.

Some readers may more readily imagine the contemporary implications of Francis' life with the assistance of a few sentences. The short paragraphs that follow the vignettes from Francis' life lead in that direction for those who find them useful.

The remarkable story of Francis is extremely provocative. Even the simplest, bare-bones portrayal of his life suggests an extraordinary power. It is a powerfully inviting contradiction to normal life—in his times and today.

The short life of Francis spanned the twelfth and thirteenth centuries. During this time the political and economic situation in Italy began to shift from feudalism to fiercely competitive city-states. A middle class was emerging, with an accompanying under class, a relationship of cause and effect that endures to this day.

Francis of Assisi embodied the purest human aspirations. Through a form of self-discipline virtually unthinkable to most of us, his gentle, deliberate move toward God drew him into that space where love abounds. For Francis, every new relationship became a joyous dance of life. From the unexpected sweetness of his life-changing embrace of a leper to the humor of his encounter with worms, from his accompaniment of beggars to his reveling in the beauties of creation, Francis entered into relationships in a way we can hardly imagine. For centuries we human beings have seen that as good—and tried to imitate him.

This book is mostly about those relationships. Each of John Swanson's pictures draws us into a relationship of Francis and how that particular relationship enhanced his relationship with

Jesus the Christ. Each picture also moves us to consider relationships in our modern world. How can we reflect on Francis preaching to the birds without being acutely aware of the damage modern societies are doing to their habitats? How can we consider Francis' deliberate steps toward poverty without remembering the millions of people in our world who live on less than a dollar a day?

This is not so much a book to nourish the intellect; rather, it is an invitation to a journey that might satisfy the soul.

Introduction
John August Swanson

Creating a painting of Saint Francis was a challenge. My first inclination was not to paint a traditional scene of Francis among animals and birds. Then I realized that one image would not be sufficient. I needed to create a fuller picture, an expanded life, rather than a single image. So I organized my sketches and developed them into miniature panels that present a biographical narrative. These twenty-four scenes form a border surrounding a central panel. I realized, as I studied this modest and heroic man, that his life was informed not by a single act but by an enormous range of experiences.

What I have attempted to do in this visual biography is capture a lifetime of experiences and events. I was reminded again and again of life's transcendent moments and that they occur and influence our growth—whether we acknowledge and recall their presence or whether they have slipped from our memory. I was also reminded that life's experiences are vastly varied. Some are quiet, offering comfort and security; others are jarring, bringing pain or loss.

For me, the motif of Francis' life is the emergence of the extraordinary out of the ordinary. Capturing the life of Francis of Assisi in a painting helped me comprehend that from the com-

monplace can emerge the significant. This is something we all share. It allowed me also to understand my life as a journey with others. Through this narrative we begin seeing the lives of people around us. We see that we all share the journey of life and that we are empowered by the acts of courage, kindness, and hope of others.

This visual biography, which combines text and art, articulates the life-long struggles of Francis' earthly journey through ridicule, ecstasy, weakness, pain, hope, and joy. Marie Dennis uses the narrative scenes in my painting of Francis as a backdrop for her reflections, which enliven this quiet saint. She suggests that in both past and present he is a hero, mentor, and spiritual companion, a human being from the thirteenth century who is a spiritual guide in the twenty-first century. In the person of Francis, who is both meek and powerful, we find a fascinating human who lives out the paradox: "God has chosen the foolish so as to embarrass the wise, God has chosen the meek so as to embarrass the powerful." Marie's text reveals the humanness of the saint as he falters along life's road, yet she also records his almost celestial desire to be extraordinary in deed and attitude.

In the end, both text and art draw us to Francis' stalwart courage, tender compassion, simple ways, and his profound desire to empower others for service and community. Francis becomes a key to understand and appreciate those lives of outstanding service around us. He reminds us through a myriad of acts and attitudes that we should serve the great human family of which we are all a part.

SAINT FRANCIS

FRANCIS OF ASSISI WAS THE
SON OF A PROSPEROUS FAMILY

Son of a Prosperous Family

Almost up to the twenty-fifth year of his age he squandered and wasted his time miserably. Indeed he outdid all his contemporaries in vanities and he came to be a promoter of evil and was more abundantly zealous for all kinds of foolishness. He was the admiration of all and strove to out do the rest in the pomp of vainglory, in jokes, in strange doings, in idle and useless talk, in songs and soft and flowering garments, for he was very rich, not however avaricious but prodigal. . . . And thus overwhelmed by a host of evil companions, proud and high-minded, he walked about the streets of Babylon. . . .

(THOMAS OF CELANO, ST. FRANCIS OF ASSISI, FIRST LIFE, I, 6)

*F*rancis of Assisi, ultimately a man of poverty and asceticism, stands pampered and protected, his feet firmly planted on the solid ground of prosperity; surrounded by the trappings of wealth; secure in the bosom of his family; sheltered from the harsh and beautiful reality of life.

Born in Assisi in 1182, Francis was the son of a wealthy cloth merchant, Pietro Bernardone, and a French woman, the Lady Pica. During those last years of the twelfth century and the beginning of the next, the Renaissance was on the distant horizon in Italy. Feudalism was just beginning to wane and a middle class was emerging. The long evolution toward the modern world was underway.

At first Francis reveled in the relative prosperity of middle-class existence. He embraced an apparently empty life with vigor and seemed blind to the underside of rising affluence. His first biographer, Thomas of Celano, painted a harsh picture of what within a few years was an already distant past:

The "streets of Babylon," paved with the trappings of wealth, separated Francis in his early years from the relationships that would later nourish his life—relationships with the vulnerable of creation, human and other, through whom he would so gloriously praise our God.

In this scene Francis has yet to choose discipleship; he has yet to hear the persistent invitation to follow the One whose voice he could not later resist; he was yet to become the icon of the icon of

God. How often we do the same, filling our days with the clutter of activity and the accumulated weight of possession!

Francis of Assisi began his journey in a place of privilege. His witness, then, is especially pertinent for those of us who also have access to abundance. Francis eventually discovered that he could not bear the separation that was wrought by his wealth, wrought by the pursuit of superficial satisfaction. He could not bear separation from the Good. An exciting but hollow existence demanded response.

Where are we in our world? What separates us from the love of God, the embrace of the leper, the doing of justice, care for creation? What have we to learn from Francis' own experience of "having much"? How would he evaluate our life?

Francis Rides Off to the Local Wars

Now Francis was soon shown in a vision a splendid palace in which he saw various military apparatus and a most beautiful bride. In the dream Francis was called by name and enticed by the promise of all these things. He attempted, therefore, to go to Apulia to win knighthood; and after he had made the necessary preparations in a lavish manner he hurried on to gain that degree of military honors. (CELANO, SECOND LIFE, II, 139)

FRANCIS RIDES OFF TO THE LOCAL WARS

*F*oolish with dreams of adventure and chivalry, Francis responds to the siren call of drama and dedication. At age 20, handsome, secure, invulnerable, he rode off to champion Assisi in its skirmish with Perugia. (How strange to imagine Assisi, now known—because of Francis—as a place for peacemaking, engaged in battle!) Elegantly attired and serene, he cannot have maintained this demeanor for long. For even small wars in beautiful countries are miserable, fierce, bloody, and painful; all captures are frightening and frustrating; all prisons, confining, claustrophobic, devoid of hospitality.

Francis, the "knight-errant," beaten down by prison life, returned home to a sick bed and a year of searching his soul. A depressed one-time court jester confronted the reality of his superficial life and yearned for a Word of invitation to faithful discipleship.

How painful conversion can be! How uncertain are times of great transition! How difficult to change the expected course of life, even for a young person! In this scene, Francis was still chasing shadows and empty promises of fame and honor.

How many of us ride off "into battle" only to discover the emptiness of our pursuits? Success for Francis meant Assisi's victory over Perugia and personal glory. In our time, success is much more likely to be defined by position or income or status or fame. What battles have we entered to encounter defeat? In what prisons have we found ourselves bound? What would it take for us to heed a different call?

Francis Gives His Cloak to a Beggar

Changed, therefore, but in mind, not in body . . . he strove to bend his own will to the will of God. Accordingly, he withdrew for a while from the bustle and the business of the world and tried to establish Jesus Christ dwelling within himself. . . . He was afire within himself with a divine fire and he was not able to hide outwardly the ardor of his mind; he repented that he had sinned so grievously . . . and neither the past evils nor those present gave him any delight. (CELANO, FIRST LIFE, III, 9-11)

FRANCIS GIVES HIS CLOAK TO A BEGGAR

$\mathcal{A}$h—the first step! Francis' soul was stirred and his feet responded! He began the long, long process of relinquishment, of letting go, moving out of his own world toward the world that he would soon know as blessed.

Jesus said that if someone asks for your cloak, you should give them all that you have. Here Francis begins to follow the lead of the One whose life he would eventually try to imitate so closely. But not just yet. This was a first step. The horse, symbol of affluence, is still at his side, at his service. He has not yet begun the process of separation from his own roots. Perhaps he believed that charity would suffice, that gifts to the poor from his surplus would be enough.

The beggar came into Francis' space to receive his help. Substantial houses surround them, only underscoring the security of Francis' existence—and, most likely, the vulnerability of the beneficiary of his generosity. Were these two men, coming from different planets, friends? Equals in the eyes of God, were they that to each other? Perhaps not yet, but maybe they soon would be.

What movement of the Spirit led Francis to this act of generosity? Did he consider the ultimate consequences of the journey on which he was about to embark? What emotions stirred in Francis in this moment? Fear? Frustration? Desire? Satisfaction? Curiosity? Hope? Love?

Do we create space in our lives for acts of generosity? Do we share what we have because we are part of a human community, where each one has a right to what they need for a dignified life? Are we unthinking, unfeeling in our most generous moments? Do we expect the poor to "qualify" in some way before they can take what is rightfully theirs?

HE BEGS FOR ALMS

He Begs for Alms

The holy father made use of alms begged from door to door much more willingly that those offered spontaneously. He would say that shame in begging is the enemy of salvation. . . . At times exhorting his brothers to go begging for alms, he would use these words, "Go," he said, "for at this last hour the Friars Minor have been lent to the world, that the elect might fulfill in them what will be commended by the Judge: Because as long as you did it for one of these, the least of my brethren, you did it for me."

(CELANO, SECOND LIFE, XLI, 198)

*T*he consequences of Francis' generosity have presented themselves quickly. This scene is radically different. Francis the
cloak-giver has become Francis the beggar. Francis the insider, the
generous one, has begun to walk in the shoes of the excluded ones,
the outsiders, the margin-dwellers. He has been invited to try on
the trappings of Lady Poverty. His newly enflamed desire for "wisdom better than gold and prudence more precious than silver"
(Celano, *First Life,* IV, 13) has impelled an affirmative response.

Dramatic, impulsive, foolish, passionate, Francis has sold
everything. His horse, his shoes, his fine clothes—all symbols of
status and wealth—have disappeared. He has already entered the
sacred, dilapidated space of the ones excluded by a society beginning to accumulate the trappings of upward mobility. Reversing
all that seemed natural, rejecting wealth and status and comfort,
the Povarello, a new beggar, was born.

Now he has begun to make his new life public. Is he humiliated, or does a modicum of dignity remain because he has freely
chosen this path? Is this breathtaking experience more intense for
Francis because he begs from the ones with whom—only yesterday—he feasted? Has he gone mad, they say? Surely this is not
required of disciples!

Have they gone mad—the ones who follow Francis and
Clare? Surely such a radical step is not required of all of Jesus' disciples! His "sell all you have, give to the poor and follow me" mes-
sage to the rich young man can't mean sell all you have—not in
modern terms! How would we manage without an extra coat,

extra shoes, an extra house, a car (an extra car), a computer, a savings account, a credit card (five credit cards), a portfolio of investments, a refrigerator full of food, fast food, gourmet food? Far too many people in our hungry world—as Francis discovered in his—involuntarily do!

HE EMBRACES THE LEPER

32

He Embraces the Leper

So greatly loathsome was the sight of lepers to him at one time, he used to say, that, in the days of his vanity, he would look at their houses only from a distance of two miles and he would hold his nostrils with his hands. But now, when by the grace of the Most High he was beginning to think of holy and useful things, while he was still clad in secular garments, he met a leper one day and, made stronger than himself, he kissed him.

(CELANO, FIRST LIFE, VII, 18-19)

Now Francis comes to the crucial moment in his conversion, an embrace of one considered repulsive, untouchable, unclean.

Francis was able to move beyond the stench of leprosy, the terror of contagion, the disgusting sight of flesh decaying on a living, breathing human being. Amazing sweetness, joy, and delight were the gifts he received in exchange, and Francis was drawn more deeply into the embrace of poverty and exclusion.

"Still clad in secular garments" when he entered this encounter, Francis emerged from the leper's embrace transformed, baptized by the fire of love, gifted with the welcome of one whose only experience of life had most likely been rejection. That was the miracle of this moment: that the leper permitted Francis' embrace. What fear and perhaps anger the leper must have overcome, what courage he exhibits here!

So often we assume we are lovable and welcome. We fail to understand the audacity of these assumptions and the great act of love and generosity of the lepers we dare to embrace.

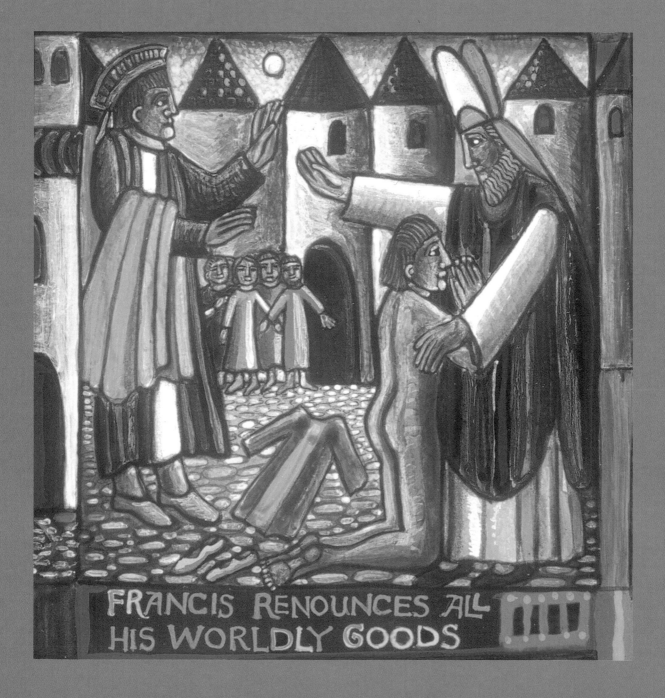

FRANCIS RENOUNCES ALL HIS WORLDLY GOODS

Francis Renounces All His Worldly Goods

When he was brought before the bishop, he would suffer no delay or hesitation in anything; indeed he did not wait for any words, nor did he speak any, but immediately putting off his clothes, and casting them aside, he gave them back to his father. (CELANO, FIRST LIFE, VI, 17)

The scene is painfully clear. Francis has not only stripped himself of his finery, but he has turned his back on his father. The anguish for both must have been searing, felt sharply, as waves of anger and sadness. The embarrassment and hurt of a son's rejection must have made the encounter unbearable for Pietro.

No longer "clad in secular clothes," Francis here is at a turning point. He had clearly been inching in this direction in his yet-young life. The burden of prosperity had become overwhelming—an obstacle to the new life he sought to embrace. And seedlings, if their roots are deep enough, can rarely be yanked out of the sod gently, especially when the sod is moss-like and choking their aspirations for new life. Then the separation is a jagged rupture, but it is necessary nonetheless.

Focused on moving beyond the boundaries that hemmed him in—and, as always, drawn to the dramatic—Francis literally and symbolically left behind everything the world told him he needed and followed a clear call to something new. Surely the most painful must have been severing the relationships that birthed and nurtured him: "Blessed are those who leave father and mother for my sake. . . !"

Francis was determined to heed the Good News as literally as possible. He simply could not remain in safe and comfortable relationships, even with the people he most loved in the world, when they prevented him from answering the unmistakable invitation of Jesus to emulate the beggars and embrace the lepers.

How ardently we reject the literal interpretation of this passage and this scene! Do we ever take any steps in that direction? Do we cling ferociously to the fine tunics in our lives and refuse repeated invitations to another Feast?

Seeking Solitude

When he prayed in the woods and in solitary places, he would fill the woods with sighs, water the places with his tears, strike his breast with his hand; and discovering there a kind of secret hiding place, he would often speak with his Lord with words. There he would give answer to his judge; there he would offer his petitions to his father; there he would talk to his friend; there he would rejoice with the bridegroom. Indeed, that he might make his whole being a holocaust in many ways, he would set before his eyes in many ways him who is simple to the greatest degree. Often, without moving his lips, he would meditate within himself and drawing external things within himself, he would lift his spirit to higher things. All his attention and affection he directed with his whole being to the one thing which he was asking of the Lord, not so much praying as becoming himself a prayer.

(Celano, Second Life, LXI, 215-216)

SEEKING SOLITUDE

*H*ow rapidly, naturally, Francis moves from a public, painful confrontation to the solace of solitude! Yearning, perhaps, for the unmediated encounter with Jesus, the Christ, who was his model, Francis here embraces another starkness—another extreme. He would move—almost rhythmically now—from insertion in, to a physical separation from, the struggles of those at the margins of a society inching its way toward the social arrangements and flaws of modernity.

The stage is set in this wilderness place for a radical encounter with his God, with the rest of creation, and with himself. Here, Francis honed his skills for attentive listening to his God, for the gentle accompaniment of a groaning creation, and for honest introspection.

Like Jesus Francis found in the desert of solitude a location to encounter life at the margins, the strength and passion to embark on his challenging mission.

He has "put on" the habit, adopting the simple brown now so characteristic of his followers, but at that time a jolting and dramatic transformation for the son of a wealthy cloth merchant. "He designed a very rough tunic that bore a likeness to the cross that by means of it he might beat off all temptations of the devil; he designed a very rough tunic that by it he might crucify the flesh with all its vices and sins; he designed a very poor and mean tunic, one that would not excite the covetousness of the world" (Celano, *First Life*, IX, 23).

In this space his rejection of all that would distract him from

discipleship was complete. He could now focus on the rebuilding of right relationships—with God, with other people, especially the most rejected and despised, and with the rest of creation.

To what solitude will we withdraw in order to make real our own commitment to new or renewed relationships? How will this move us to deeper, richer engagement at the margins of our world? What balance will we find between action and contemplation? Of what will our new tunic be made?

God's Troubadour

At times, as we saw with our own eyes, he would pick up a stick from the ground and putting it over his left arm would draw across it, as across a violin a little bow bent by means of a string. And going through the motions of playing, he would sing in French about his Lord. This whole ecstasy of joy would often end in tears and his song of gladness would be dissolved in compassion for the passion of Christ. (CELANO, SECOND LIFE, XC, 242)

GOD'S TROUBADOR

SISTERS MOON
AND STARS

BROTHER WIND

*M*usic. What role could music possibly have played in the life of the poor man from Assisi? Isn't poverty somber? Hadn't he moved beyond the places of frolic and merriment that he used to inhabit? Could there be joy where he now dwells?

Before Francis moved his lot to the side of the poor—before his conversion—he was a singer of songs, a balladeer, a bard. Outgoing and popular before he traded his elegant wardrobe for rough brown beggar's rags, Francis sang songs to amuse his social set, perhaps to play the part of a fool. Now he has become a fool for Christ and he is singing a new song.

Surely it is a song of praise that lifts his spirit. Perhaps it offers a glimmer of the canticle he will later write after deep, deep suffering has scored his soul. The sun, the earth, and her creatures revel in the beauty of sounds that give glory to the Source of All Being, the Spirit of Life.

Could the song be an invitation as well, a gentle enticement to those who would follow? The life I have chosen, it said, is profoundly happy. Come. Taste and see. Here I have found the goodness of the Lord. The sweetness I tasted as I embraced the leper has endured. Even the bitterness of poverty, the exhaustion of grueling physical work, the humiliation of begging have not erased the gift of that joy. It can be yours as well.

Do we dare to believe it? Is that promise too old to buy? What will it cost me to try it? My way of life? My security? Empty pleasures? Can I also learn to sing a new song?

Followers Join Him in Doing Good Works

They came together with great desire; they remained together with joy. . . . Followers of most holy poverty, because they had nothing, loved nothing, they feared in no way to lose anything. They were content with one tunic, patched at times within and without; in it was seen no refinement, but rather abjectness and cheapness, so that they might seem to be completely crucified to the world. Girt with a cord, they wore poor trousers and they had the pious intention of remaining like this and they wished to have nothing more.

(CELANO, FIRST LIFE, XV, 37)

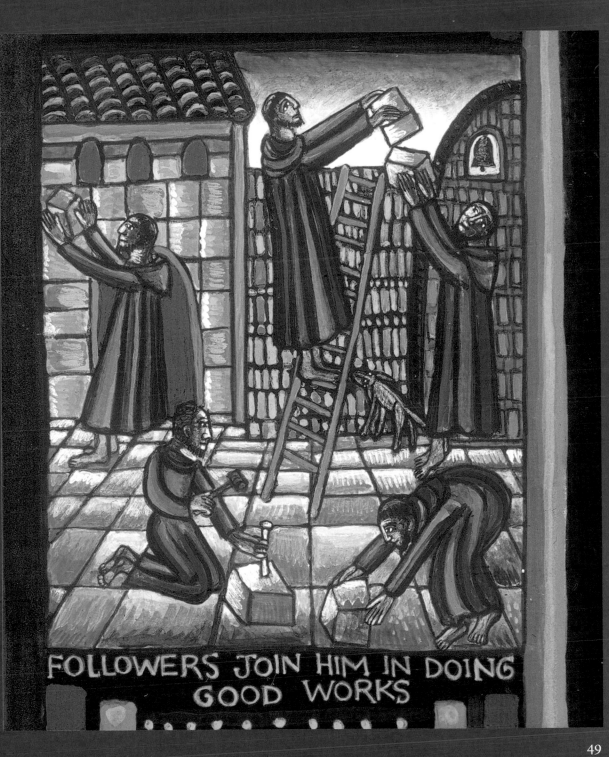

FOLLOWERS JOIN HIM IN DOING GOOD WORKS

The Franciscan community begins to gather. The life of Francis, the gently, joyful way of poverty—strange as it may seem—proved irresistible. First the brothers followed, imitating his way. Moving to the margins of Assisi society, they too accom-

panied the poor, the outcasts. They embraced a life of intense austerity, rejecting every privilege and every modicum of security. Decidedly not clerics, they chose instead the egalitarian, even subservient life of brothers. Deeply religious, faithful followers of Jesus, they broke open the only mold for religious life in their times. Rejecting the stability of place, they had no monastery, no treasure, no roots. They became paupers, panhandlers, mendicants, workers in the house of God.

With different dispositions and personalities they came, and willed themselves into a community following Francis, following Jesus. Exchanging whatever manner of clothing they had, some fine and others not so fine, they donned the common rough cloth of the poor. Setting aside whatever privilege or position they had, they took up the tools of their new trade and set their hearts and their backs on a challenging journey together.

What attraction did this way of life have for the first Franciscans? Perhaps, in the sterility of an increasingly prosperous society or the drudgery of an ordinary early thirteenth-century life, it was community itself that drew the multitudes.

How easily we can identify! We too yearn for community, for a common life that nurtures and challenges and supports us in our own efforts to be faithful disciples. In fact, it is the infectious and radical individualism that too often defines the assumptions about "normal" life that impels our pursuit of the companionship of community. And, today, community is sometimes not so easy to find.

Taming the Wolf of Gubbio

Weakened and consumed by his extreme mortifications, watchings, prayers and fasting, St. Francis was unable to travel on foot and was carried by donkey when he could not walk and especially after he was marked with the wounds of the Saviour.

And late one evening while he was riding on a donkey along the San Verecondo road with a companion, wearing a coarse sack over his shoulders, some farm workers called to him, saying, "Brother Francis, stay here with us and don't go farther, because some fierce wolves are running around here, and they will devour your donkey and hurt you too."

Then St. Francis said, "I have not done any harm to Brother Wolf that he should dare to devour our Brother Donkey. Good-bye, my sons, and fear God."

So St. Francis went on his way. And he was not hurt.

(Brown, 321)

TAMING THE WOLF OF GUBBIO

rancis's sensitivity to the rest of creation quickly became legendary. In later versions of this legend, the wild beast terrorizing the city of Gubbio became docile at the beckoning of Francis. Through respectful interaction with a creature feared by everyone, Francis resolved a potentially dangerous situation. The enemy of the whole village was changed when the hunger that drove his marauding was assuaged. Francis' instinct for addressing violence by understanding its root causes served him—and the community—very well. And his open encounter with the wolf enabled its destructive instincts to be transformed.

Courageous encounters with the wolves of this age have accomplished or promise relief from the impact of evil. Truth commissions and tribunals in many countries have exposed human rights abusers to international scrutiny and condemnation. Survivors of torture have stopped the torment by naming those responsible. Apartheid finally succumbed to global outrage. But too many wolves—racism, xenophobia, homophobia and more—continue to roam unacknowledged in our souls and institutions and unconfronted by our societies.

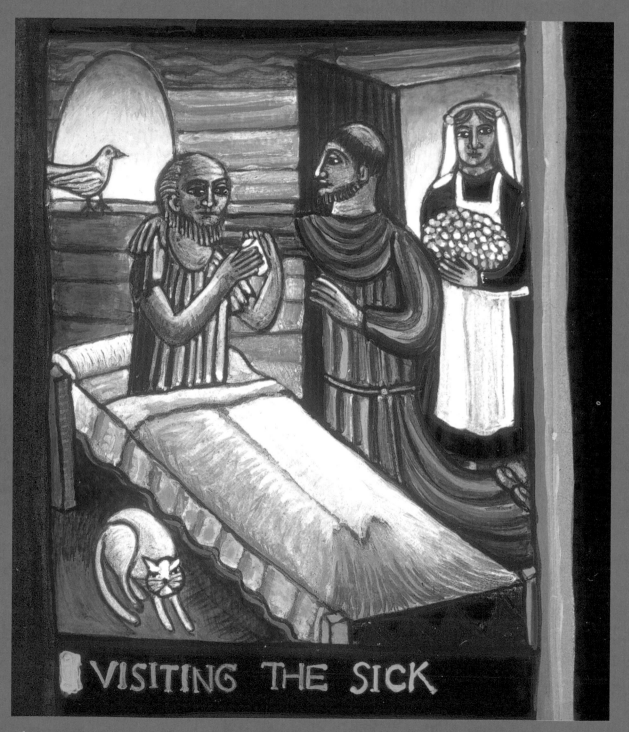

VISITING THE SICK

Visiting the Sick

Francis had great compassion for the sick, great concern for their needs. When the kindness of secular people sent him choice foods, even though he needed them more than others, he gave them to the rest of the sick. He transferred to himself the afflictions of all who were sick, offering them words of sympathy when he could not give them help. . . . But he admonished the ill to bear their troubles patiently and not to give scandal when all their wishes were not satisfied. . . . (CELANO, SECOND LIFE, CXXXIII, 277)

*I*ntensely engaged in nurturing his relationship with a God both transcendent and incarnate, Francis' journey is said to have mirrored Jesus' own. The sick, the hungry, the homeless, the lonely, the forgotten dwelt at the center of his stage.

From the clamor of voices petitioning Francis to heal their afflictions, the holy man singled out one after another to gift with his caring and compassionate attention. Multiple stories give testimony to the gentle care he offered broken bodies.

Francis' encounter with the sick and the wounded was intrinsically reciprocal. He gave to them generously of his attention and healing power, but he also drew from them something foundational to his own life's project. "Then the holy lover of complete humility went to the lepers and lived with them, serving them most diligently for God's sake, and washing all foulness from them, he wiped away also the corruption of the ulcer . . ." (Celano, *First Life*, VII, 18).

Out of this encounter Francis' healing power became one that touched the body and the community and the spirit as well, persistently leading it toward the One Who Loves All. Time and again Francis reminded the one restored to physical wholeness that restoration of life to the soul was as necessary as a cure for physical illness or disability—without it, the body would soon again decay.

He healed the sick out of great kindness, but he cured their ills principally to make the healing of the whole person more possible. Death of the body was not to be feared, but embraced as a sister; death of the spirit was what ought to terrify.

Life in these times underscores our obsession with values opposite to those that led Francis to his healing ministry. Everything around us suggests that death is to be avoided at all costs—that perpetual restoration of our bodily functions (or appearance) is the ultimate good. We spend fortunes on creams and potions and empty promises because we cannot believe what Francis knew.

Preaching to the Fish

Once when he was sitting in a boat near a port in the Lake of Rieti, a certain fisherman, who had caught a big fish popularly called a tinca, offered it kindly to him. He accepted it joyfully and kindly began to call it brother; then, placing it in the water outside the boat, he began devoutly to bless the name of the Lord. And while he continued in prayer for some time, the fish played in the water beside the boat and did not go away from the place where it had been put until his prayer was finished and the holy man of God gave it permission to leave.

(CELANO, FIRST LIFE, XXI, 56)

PREACHING TO THE FISH

*K*neeling, Francis preaches from a place of humility, acknowledging the common heritage of all God's handiwork, human and not. He moves close to the easily frightened, beautiful water creatures gently, honoring their nature and bridging the gap between them and the ones who have consistently harvested their lives without thanks. He tells them of God's love for them and gives praise for their presence that so beautifies the earth.

Francis' way of life so often approaches the absurd! Imagine a man called holy, whose life ultimately attracted millions of followers, on his knees preaching to the fish! Surely few have achieved the depth of the Povarello's integration. His wholehearted embrace of the divine self-gift, his ravenous appetite for the Good News, and his awareness of God's presence in creation, imbuing every living being with profound dignity and worth, made sense of this simple, foolish act.

Is the long journey of human creatures finally turning toward the rest of creation? Will we soon be able to understand what Francis seemed to intuit over eight hundred years ago? Faced with the danger of her utter destruction, will we look with new eyes at the spectacular richness represented by other life on this planet? Will we begin to treat the other with respect?

VISITING PRISONERS

Visiting Prisoners

Indeed, once when there was a bloody battle between the citizens of Perugia and those of Assisi, Francis was made captive with several others and endured the squalors of prison. His fellow captives were consumed with sorrow, bemoaning miserably their imprisonment; Francis rejoiced in the Lord, laughed at his chains and despised them.

(Celano, Second Life, I, 138)

*H*ighlighting again the pastoral nature of his ministry, Francis makes real another of the corporal works of mercy in a manner that seems entirely ordinary. The brown-robed visitor, however, has uncanny sensitivity to the suffering of those in prison, for he himself spent time behind bars. Reaching out to those deprived of interaction with family and loved ones, Francis cheers the prisoners and restores their hope in God's love.

So often prisons were filled not only with criminals, equally loved by God, but also by the most forgotten, the poorest of people, the ones to whom Francis was repeatedly drawn. He would have had enormous compassion for these five—perhaps they were friends from the street, or lepers who had overstepped their bounds. Perhaps they reminded Francis of the imprisoned ones to whom Jesus announced the Year of God's Favor, or the friends of Jesus imprisoned repeatedly for preaching the same Good News.

In our times prison bars have again become a symbol of oppression. Too many impoverished people, too many seeking justice, too many abandoned by society, too many children find themselves confined by walls and bars and barbed wire. Too many who are broken find themselves threatened again by a system that demands their last ounce of flesh. Too many are tortured and abused. Too many accused but never found guilty find themselves secreted away in clandestine cells. Too many who need mental health care instead are given prison terms. Now this corporal work of mercy demands accompaniment by the work for restorative justice and respect for basic human rights!

"Our Sisters the Birds
Are Singing God's Praises"

He came to a certain place near Bevagna where a very great number of birds of various kinds had congregated, namely, doves, crows, and some others popularly called daws. When the most blessed servant of God, Francis, saw them, being a man of very great fervor and great tenderness toward lower and irrational creatures, he left his companions in the road and ran eagerly toward the birds. When he was close enough to them, seeing that they were waiting expectantly for him, he greeted them in his usual way. But, not a little surprised that the birds did not rise in flight, as they usually do, he was filled with great joy and humbly begged them to listen to the word of God.

(Celano, First Life, XXI, 54-55)

OUR SISTERS THE BIRDS
ARE · SINGING · GOD'S PRAISES

*H*ere Francis joins the chorus of praise already resounding. Perhaps there is a purity of tone, a simplicity of melody that invites the man of God to listen. His clear, direct communication with other creatures honors their worth and invites right relationship. He recognizes the lovely melody as one that truly honors the Creator God and his whole body appreciatively joins the song of praise.

Francis' awareness of God's presence seemed constant. His sense of God's great love for all of creation made him see the value of the simplest living thing. Francis believed that the lovely, intricate handiwork of the Creator was endowed with dignity and worth simply because it was and, because of that dignity, had the capacity to give glory to God. Without detracting from the worth of human creation, Francis could revel in the wonder of all that surrounded him.

If only Francis' insights about the value of all creation were able to inform the world's decisions about human interaction with the natural order now. His relationships with animals and nature that inspired awe in the thirteenth century and seem like foolishness in the modern era could become a survival guide for a distressed planet.

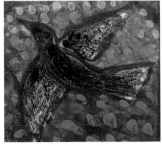

Feeding the Hungry

One night one of the sheep cried out while the rest were sleeping, "I am dying brothers, I am dying of hunger." Immediately, the good shepherd got up and hastened to give the ailing sheep the proper remedy. He commanded the table to be set, though it was filled with poor things, and, as is often the case, where wine was lacking water took its place. First, he himself began to eat, and then he invited the rest of the brothers to share this duty of charity, lest that brother should waste away from shame.

(CELANO, SECOND LIFE, XV, 154)

FEEDING THE HUNGRY

*F*rancis again becomes servant to one in need. His compassionate attention to his hungry brother mirrored his compassionate commitment to the ones always forgotten by society. He fed the hungry, including the brother, because he knew them as human beings who deserved a life of dignity. "To deprive the body indiscreetly of what it needs," he said, "was a sin just the same as it is a sin to give it superfluous things at the prompting of gluttony" (Celano, *Second Life,* XV, 155).

Francis had walked in the shoes of the hungry; he had accompanied them on the streets of Assisi; he had begged at their side for his own sustenance; he had disciplined his own body by regular fasting and knew well the pain of hunger. He had rejected a life of prosperity and plenty in order to share their lot. But he always sought to honor the dignity of the hungry one.

Francis also fed the hungry because Jesus fed the hungry. He invited hungry beloveds to the table of life and served them there in imitation of Jesus, whose word was about one loaf to be shared by all and whose practice of inclusive community led ultimately to the cross.

In these times, feeding the hungry carries enormous social, political and economic weight. We need to be asking, who is seated at our tables? Who raises our food and how? Who prepares and serves our meals and how are they treated? What is their place at the table? Do we have more than we need for today? Do we ever say enough? What do we eat? How many of our meals do justice? How many nourish both body and soul?

"Brother Donkey, Your Virtues Are Hard Work and Patience"

Finally, he called all creatures brother and in a most extraordinary manner, a manner never experienced by others, he discerned the hidden things of nature with his sensitive heart, as one who had already escaped into the freedom of the glory of the sons [and daughters] of God.

(CELANO, FIRST LIFE, XXIX, 73)

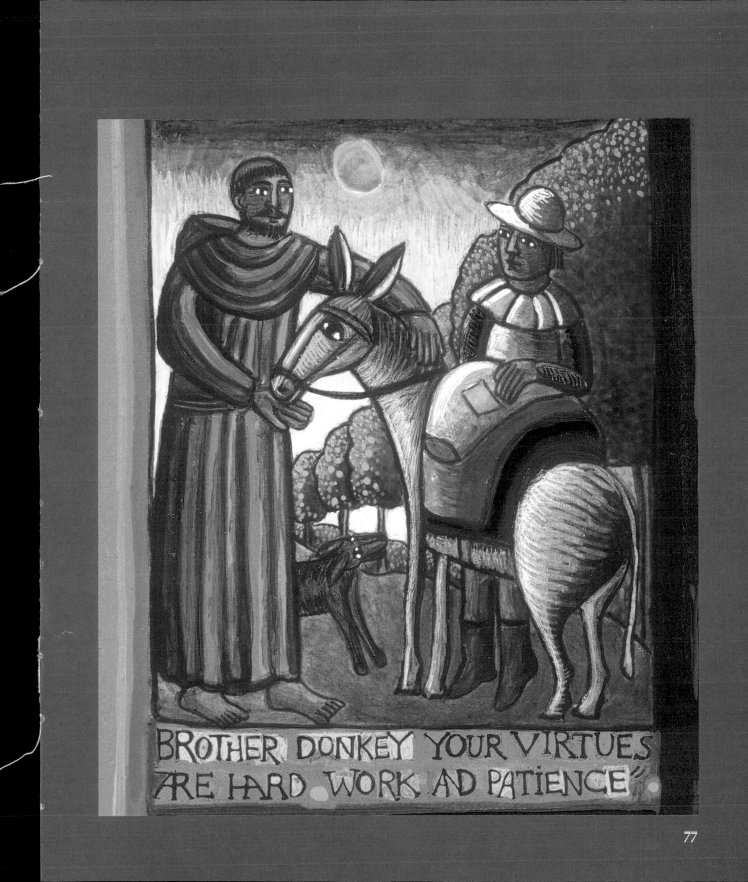

Francis approaches the hard-working creature and embraces him with the fondness of a treasured friend. Time pauses, tasks and errands of the day are interrupted for a momentary encounter beyond the understanding of most human beings.

Once again Francis demonstrates his capacity to appreciate the gifts and contributions to life of those struggling in the background of the human drama. Beasts of burden, part of the scenery of everyday life in Francis' time, were necessary and functional, but probably rarely noticed. The sensitivities of the saint were finely tuned; his pace of life was deliberate enough, and his focus clear enough that he saw the effort of the heavily laden animal.

Significantly, the virtues Francis extols in brother ass reveal much about his own values. He could have been talking to one of his brothers, or to his own body, for all followers of Francis were expected to earn their daily bread with patient and servile work. To place oneself alongside the most burdened ones was to accompany the most impoverished human beings. Their work was often unnoticed, unappreciated, unrewarded, but essential nonetheless to the survival of the wealthy and powerful.

The scenery of everyday life in our own times is not so very different. In many places, four-legged beasts of burden continue the patient hard work that has been their lot, but everywhere unpaid or underpaid human beasts of burden—farm workers, factory workers, sex workers, household workers, miners, and millions more—carry for the world a workload that is unjust.

THE PEACEMAKER

The Peacemaker

Coming therefore to Perugia, he began to preach to the people who had gathered about; but when some knights rode up on their horses, as is their custom, and crossing their weapons in a military exercise, interfering with his words, the saint turned to them and sighing, said, "O miserable folly of wretched men, who do not consider nor fear the judgment of God! But listen to what the Lord announces to you through me, poor little one. The Lord," he said, "has exalted you above all others around you; for this reason you should be kinder to your neighbors and you should live in a way more pleasing to God. But, ungrateful for God's grace, you attack your neighbors with arms, kill and plunder them. I say to you: this will not go unpunished. . . .

(CELANO, SECOND LIFE, VIII, 169-170)

*F*rancis' impetus to make peace bore ample fruit. Here he enters fully and physically into the task of peacemaking, embracing quite literally the combatants, insisting that the tools of violence be transformed. His deepest beliefs in the value of each life, his own painful experience of war, and his commitment to follow Jesus made of him a determined and effective peacemaker.

His approach was surely neither superficial nor one that assiduously avoided conflict. In fact, Francis must have often created conflict—remember his confrontation with his father. Perhaps his effectiveness as a peacemaker emerged from his willingness to enter conflictive situations—even to take on the violence himself as Jesus did—in order to find lasting peace. His visit to the sultan during the Crusades surely could not have been popular with Christians willing to give their lives and kill others (the crux of the matter for Francis) in defense of their faith—or so they were told. Francis accepted their wrath but continued to try to bridge tremendous geographical, cultural and religious differences to encounter "the enemy" as a human being worthy of respect.

Like Jesus, Francis broke down barriers between neighbors and nations and religious beliefs. "Many who had hated peace, and had hated also salvation, embraced peace" (Celano, *First Life*, X, 24). His witness is a powerful one, for we have many such divisions in our times—divisions that protect privilege and power and wealth, that hide insecurity and fear, and that contribute in a mighty way to the lack of peace that surrounds us.

WELCOMING THE HOMELESS

Welcoming the Homeless

When he was on a pilgrimage to Rome, he put off his fine garments out of love of poverty, clothed himself with the garments of a certain poor man, and joyfully sat among the poor in the vestibule before the church of St. Peter, where there were many poor, and considering himself one of them, he ate eagerly with them. Many times he would have done a similar thing had he not been held back by shame before those who knew him.

(CELANO, SECOND LIFE, IV, 142)

*I*n this scene Francis welcomes the homeless, which he undoubtedly did many, many times—always as equals, because they were also God's children. He welcomed them as friends because he knew them or their brothers and sisters on the streets. He welcomed them as Christ because he had gone into the streets to find Jesus among them—and he had.

Francis' personal journey toward a new life followed a circuitous path. Many key elements of that conversion were variations on the same theme—one of a rich man moving deliberately to the side of Lazarus. Francis embraced a leper, then befriended lepers; he gave away all that he had and took up begging to survive; he joined the homeless on the streets of Rome, was welcomed by them, and welcomed in return.

When Francis was with the poor ones outside of St. Peter's, he noted the "meager offerings" of those who responded to the pleas of the hungry and homeless and was ashamed. The lens through which he viewed reality was a new one and everything looked dramatically different.

How often do we walk past homeless people, never noticing or acknowledging their humanity, never attempting to honor their dignity? What would it require of us to be present to them, accompany them, to know them as human beings with interesting and important stories for us to hear? What would happen if we tried to look at life in our times through the eyes of those who now are hungry and homeless?

Freeing the Captives

When the blessed Francis was going across the lake . . . a certain fisherman offered him a waterfowl, that he might rejoice over it in the Lord. The blessed father accepted it joyfully, and opening his hands, he gently told it that it was free to fly away. But when it did not wish to leave but wanted to rest there in his hands as in a nest, the saint raised his eyes and remained in prayer. And returning to himself as from another place after a long while, he gently commanded the bird to go back to its former freedom. So, upon receiving this permission along with a blessing, the bird flew away, showing its joy by a certain movement of the body. (CELANO, SECOND LIFE, CXXVI, 272)

FREEING THE CAPTIVES

*H*ow far we have come from imagining the gentle, winged creatures around us as captives! Francis immediately saw this fundamental insult to their very nature and acted in response. The plight of these lovely creatures made by God to soar, to fly freely beyond the reach of danger, would have been instantly recognized by many indigenous people whose vision and sensitivity mirror that of St. Francis. We may be invited to fly with our sister and brother creatures, but we cannot deprive them of that which comprises their very nature. They, like we, are called to the fullness of being!

The young man being approached by Francis would probably have been dumbfounded to discover that he could not possess the birds, that he could not possess their beauty or their life, that he could not own the treasures of creation but only delight in their loveliness. The excessive accumulation by wealthy societies changes this fact not a bit. We cannot possess beauty or life. And the attempt to do so that is often the promise and lure of the global marketplace leaves many human spirits captive to consumerism and greed, overwhelmed by the weight of unnecessary possessions, while others are choked by the absence of the barest necessities.

The human spirit, so attracted to these creatures filled with life, is afraid to let them go, lest we lack the freedom to soar with them. Imprisoned by wealth and power, poverty and violence, intolerance or racism, oppression or fear, we hold on too tightly, we lock the gate and cover the cage, because the responsibilities of freedom are overwhelming.

How can we return to the place of delight promised to us? How can we ensure that others can be there as well? How can we shed the shackles that weigh us down so that we can learn from and enjoy what we cannot possess? How can we release the captives that we hold fast by blindness and greed?

Caring for Orphans

Another time . . . he met a certain man who had two little lambs hanging bound over his shoulder, taking them to the market to sell them. When blessed Francis heard them bleating, he was filled with pity; and, coming close, he touched them and showed his compassion for them like a mother over her weeping child. And he said to the man: "Why are you torturing my brother lambs tied up and hanging like this?" Answering, he said, "I am taking them to the market to sell them because I need the money." The saint said, "What will happen to them then?" He answered, "Those who buy them will kill them and eat them." "God forbid," replied the saint; "this must not happen. Take the mantle I am wearing as their price and give the lambs to me." (CELANO, FIRST LIFE, XXVIII, 71)

CARING FOR ORPHANS

*I*n the time of Francis, orphans may well have been naturally cared for by family or community, but those who had neither may well have found Francis' austere lifestyle familiar and his hard working, loving community a place of security. Perhaps Clare and her sisters found a corner of their convent for little ones from time to time—surely that has been a Franciscan-Clariana charism ever since.

Today abandoned children, by their sheer numbers, overwhelm the most generous attentions of caring individuals. Street children flee from poverty into deeper poverty—from Brazil to India to Guatemala; from Zimbabwe to Nicaragua. Begging in extremely dangerous situations for long hours, young ones sniff glue to dull the hunger or quiet the fear. Often threatened or killed by unsympathetic police or sold into prostitution, orphans from AIDS are now swelling their ranks.

How many Bachs or Einsteins, Romeros or Nelson Mandelas perish on the streets of our world before they even reach the age of reason? And what can we do to help?

CLARE OF ASSISI ASKS TO FOLLOW THE LIFE OF POVERTY AND PRAYER

Clare of Assisi Asks to Follow the Life of Poverty and Prayer

For when, after the beginning of the Order of Brothers, the said lady was converted to God through the counsel of the holy man, she lived unto the advantage of many and as an example to a countless multitude. She was noble of parentage, but she was more noble by grace; she was a virgin in body, most chaste in mind; a youth in age, but mature in spirit; steadfast in spirit and most ardent in her desire for divine love; endowed with wisdom and excelling in humility; Clare by name, brighter in life and brightest in character. (CELANO, FIRST LIFE, VIII, 20)

*F*rancis welcomes the woman who would have such an impact on the community, then just beginning to gather. Clare and her sisters embraced the life wholeheartedly. Like Francis, she gave up comfort and security to embrace a radical life of poverty and prayer. Her sister, and eventually her mother, followed. A woman of great strength, she became a dear friend of Francis, and clearly his equal in vision and commitment. Clare and the women who accompanied her as she walked with Francis brought a steady and profound challenge to the community's life.

Many believe that the women's way of poverty was even more stark that that of the brothers. Surely the walls of their convent limited their ability to support themselves—even by begging. Their vulnerability was profound, yet Clare insisted that the rule of radical poverty be maintained. No property would be owned, no security guaranteed. Bound by forms of religious life then the norm in many ways, they carved a path of poverty inside the boundaries as radical as was Francis' outside.

Many accounts illustrate Clare's vision and persistence—the rule for her community was approved only after years of effort on her part—but also her humanity. One of the loveliest legends about Clare describes her determination to share a meal with Francis, as his friend, and of her success in doing so, in the company of others from their communities. On that occasion the fire of friendship in the Spirit lit up the sky for all of Assisi to behold: "But when they reached the Place they found that nothing was on fire. Entering the Place, they found St. Francis and St. Clare and all

the companions sitting around that very humble table, rapt in God by contemplation and invested with power from on high. Then they knew for sure that it had been a heavenly and not a material fire that God had miraculously shown them to symbolize the fire of divine love which was burning in the souls of those holy friars and nuns . . ." (Brown, 73).

The witness of Francis and Clare to friendship rooted in radical discipleship, equality, and community gives modern disciples nourishing food for thought. Do our friendships, our relationships, deepen and encourage our commitments to God and to a better world, or do they take us to places less noble?

The Vision of God Touches
Francis in a Special Way

Two years before Francis gave his soul back to heaven, while he was living in the hermitage which was called Alverna, after the place on which it stood, he saw in the vision of God a man standing above him, like a seraph with six wings, his hands extended and his feet joined together and fixed to a cross. . . . When the blessed servant of the Most High saw these things, he was filled with the greatest wonder, but he could not understand what this vision should mean. Still, he was filled with happiness and he rejoiced very greatly . . . but the fact that the seraph was fixed to a cross and the sharpness of his suffering filled Francis with fear. And so he arose, if I may so speak, sorrowful and joyful, and joy and grief were in him alternately. . . . And while he was thus unable to come to any understanding of it and the strangeness of the vision perplexed his heart, the marks of the nails began to appear in his hands and feet, just as he had seen them a little before in the crucified man above him. (CELANO, FIRST LIFE, III, 84-85)

*I*n many ways this scene may be the most central to understanding this still-young man from Assisi. More often imagined preaching to the birds or perhaps caring for the poor, Francis is not usually pictured at this moment of intense joy and suffering. This extraordinary encounter with a seraphic messenger fulfilled Francis' passionate desire to walk, as literally as possible, in Jesus' footsteps, and left him forever bearing the wounds of Christ. Just as Jesus on his way to and on the cross carried the sufferings of our world, so did Francis desire to assume them. For the last years of his life, as he bore the stigmata, Francis suffered intensely, and in the suffering he seemed to experience great joy.

This is a strange encounter by all modern standards. What led Francis to this moment was his dedicated imitation of Christ. His desire for physical identification with the sufferings of Christ thrust him not into the realm of the spirit but deeply into the broken and bleeding world of the real.

Like Jesus, he fully embraced the messy, painful, broken human journey—not only to feed or comfort or heal or accompany, but to challenge social structures and practices that ostracized, humiliated, deprived, and battered life at every turn. For his trouble Jesus was given the death penalty. Francis shared that cross by which Jesus redeemed the world, accompanying the wounded ones who bear in their flesh the consequences of greed and injustice, violence and war.

The paradoxes of life through death and joy through suffering give lie to some of the deepest held beliefs of modern life. How in these times and our lives do we make sense of this scene?

Composing the Canticle of Praise

Be praised, my Lord, with all your creatures,
Especially Sir Brother Sun,
By whom you give us the light of day!
And he is beautiful and radiant with great splendor.
Of You, Most High, he is a symbol!

Be praised, my Lord, for Sister Moon and the Stars!
In the sky you formed them bright and lovely and fair.

Be praised, my Lord, for Brother Wind
And for the Air and cloudy and clear and all Weather
By which You give sustenance to your creatures!

Be praised, my Lord, for Sister Water,
Who is very useful and humble and lovely and chaste!

Be praised, my Lord, for Brother Fire,
By whom you give us light at night,
And he is beautiful and merry and mighty and strong!

Be praised, my Lord, for our Sister Mother Earth,
Who sustains and governs us,
And produces fruits with colorful flowers and leaves!

(BROWN, 317)

BROTHER SUN · SISTER WATER · MOTHER EARTH

SISTER'S MOON AND STARS · BROTHER FIRE

CANTICLE OF THE SUN
FRANCIS

BROTHER WIND · SISTER DEATH

*F*ranciscan historians suggest that the saint wrote this magnificent song when he was in tremendous physical pain. His eyesight had deteriorated; he was almost blind—yet he could revel in the wonder of creation and sing the praises of the Source of All Being. He seemed to have the gift of anticipatory delight in the New Creation. He felt in his soul the kinship, the intrinsic interconnection of human beings and the rest of creation. In the Canticle he revealed the essence of the Franciscan worldview— "that God is the Source of all being. The Creator God is the Parent, both Mother and Father of all creatures, who are therefore brother and sister to one another. Because all of creation is part of this divine family, everything created, animate and inanimate, deserves brotherly and sisterly love and respect" (Dennis, 109).

Despite growing ecological sensitivity in these times, Creation is still abused and polluted, especially through lifestyles of affluence and waste. Sister Water, Brothers Wind and Air, Sister Earth are not commodities to be exploited for profit but manifestations of God's continued and creative presence.

Francis invites us to right relationship with the rest of creation, to repent of our sin of domination, and to actively participate in works of environmental healing.

In the Year 1226 Francis Dies among His Brothers

Then he spent the few days that remained before his death in praise, teaching his companions whom he loved so much to praise Christ with him. . . . He also invited all creatures to praise God, and by means of the words he had composed earlier, he exhorted them to love God. He exhorted death itself, terrible and hateful to all, to give praise, and going joyfully to meet it, he invited it to make its lodging with him. "Welcome," he said, "my sister death. . . ." Then to the brothers, "When you see that I am brought to my last moments, place me naked upon the ground just as you saw me the day before yesterday; and let me lie there after I am dead for the length of time it takes one to walk a mile unhurriedly." The hour therefore came, and all the mysteries of Christ being fulfilled in him, he winged his way happily to God.

(CELANO, SECOND BOOK, CLXIII, 311)

IN THE YEAR 1226 FRANCIS
DIES AMONG HIS BROTHERS

*E*very year on October 3, Franciscans around the world retell the story of their founder's death. In memorial services called the Transitus, details of his passing into new life are remembered with great reverence.

Events that preceded the scene in this picture are significant. Francis was most specific in his instructions to his community. He had suffered intensely from a long illness and approached death with joy. Francis eagerly anticipated the arrival of Sister Death when he would finally move into the embrace of the One he had so long pursued. Truly a "hound of heaven," Francis tolerated the burden of earthly existence, yet persistently practiced the disciplines that kept him detached. Or was he?

For a man so intent upon embracing death, the brother from Assisi immersed himself thoroughly in the messy carnal reality around him and reached an identity with the rest of creation—from the earth to the birds to brother ass—that echoed the incarnational impetus of the God he pursued.

As death neared, Francis asked to be brought back to Assisi, stripped of his clothing and laid bare upon the bare earth, making his loving embrace of the natural world complete. For Francis, symbolic actions were enormously important—and his manner of death was true to form. Lying on the earth he loved so dearly, surrounded by his community, Francis blessed the brothers, and called them to be faithful after he was gone. How painful must have been the separation of the brothers from the women of the community at that time! Immediately after his death, according to Thomas of Celano, the brothers carried his body to the Portiuncula so that Claire and her sisters could honor his passing.

Francis' death was cause for mourning and for celebration. Here the broken and impoverished vehicle for his great spirit is revered, the radical, inspiring witness of his life remembered. In life Francis pushed beyond all boundaries and barriers in his pursuit of holiness; he challenged the values and lifestyle of Assisi and beyond. In death his challenge continues.

Concluding Reflection

Everyone who thirsts, come to the waters;

and you that have no money, come, buy and eat!

Come, buy wine and milk, without money and without price.

Why do you spend your money for that which is not bread?

And your labor for that which does not satisfy?

Listen carefully to me, and eat what is good, and delight

      yourselves in rich food.

Incline your ear, and come to me;

Listen, so that you may live. . . .

For as the rain and the snow come down from heaven,

and do not return there until they have watered the earth,

making it bring forth and sprout,

giving seed to the sower and bread to the eater,

so shall my word be that goes out from my mouth;

it shall not return to me empty, but it shall accomplish
    that which I purpose,
and succeed in the thing for which I sent it.

For you shall go out in joy, and be led back in peace;
The mountains and the hills before you shall burst into song,
And all the trees of the field shall clap their hands.
Instead of the thorn shall come up the cypress;
Instead of the brier shall come the myrtle;
and it shall be to the Lord for a memorial,
for an everlasting sign that shall not be cut off.

(Isaiah 55: 1-3, 10-13)

Bibliography

Brown, Raphael, ed. and trans. *The Little Flowers of St. Francis* (New York: Image Books, 1958).

Dennis, Marie, Joseph Nangle, OFM, Cynthia Moe-Lobeda, and Stuart Taylor. *St. Francis and the Foolishness of God* (Maryknoll, New York: Orbis Books, 1993).

Thomas of Celano. *St. Francis of Assisi: First and Second Life* (Chicago: Franciscan Herald Press, 1963).

About Francis of Assisi

John August Swanson

When I walked through the Frick Collection in New York City in 1973, I was very taken by one of the paintings. As I stood in front of *St. Francis in Ecstasy*, painted in the late 1470s by Giovanni Bellini, I was struck by its power and its visual complexity and at the same time its simplicity. This painting stayed in my heart. Later, when reading about the life of Francis, I was also taken by the reproductions of Giotto's paintings of his life. Created in the early fourteenth century, these paintings of important events in the life of a wonderful saint and friend touched and inspired me.

I had made various sketches and isolated drawings of Saint Francis but I was never satisfied enough to begin a painting. Eventually, in 1983, I made a small painting of Francis surrounded by many kinds of standing and flying birds. The more I learned of him, the more possibilities there seemed to be. I tried many sketches, usually with Francis standing in nature surrounded by animals and birds. Although the drawings were interesting, I did not feel that they captured his spirit and life. I still was not ready to paint.

In 1983 I printed two limited edition lithographs at the studio of Efram Wolff. Both of them were biblical narratives in which I drew a frame around a central panel with many miniature scenes that related to the story. They were modest works of only a few colors. In order to work with more skill in lithography, I took a print-making class to learn techniques that are unique to lithography. In early 1985, Efram Wolff invited me to return later to work on another project. I saw this as a good opportunity to develop my ideas on Francis.

I made a series of drawings that could form a completed work. What I wanted to show was Francis' struggles and his extraordinary generosity to people. Because of the disturbing events around the world and in our own country during the mid-1980s, I felt that people needed a visual reminder of the life of a mentor and friend. I began drawing scenes that showed Francis helping, empowering, sharing, and walking with others on their journey through life. The process was exciting for me and I felt compelled to incorporate them into a more complex image, using my earlier technique of incorporating many scenes in a border around a central image.

In the spring of 1985, after showing some of my work at an exhibition in Grand Rapids, Michigan, I took the train to New York. While on the train, I continued drawing and reading accounts of Francis' life, trying to focus on what I felt was important for contemporary life. I also had to decide what I wanted to share with people of many different faiths, so that they could also be inspired by Francis. I went to the Frick Collection once more to see the Bellini painting. Its beauty helped me see Francis' place in nature, one of wonder and contemplation. It inspired me once more to portray my own vision.

I now moved with confidence as I made larger sketches,

assembling the scenes of the border that would surround the central panel. It was important to have some kind of visual logic and reference to time in the border. When I began work on the lithograph, the first plate I drew became my reference for each of the other six plates used: one plate was made for each color to be printed. Each plate took over a week to draw. After I finished it, the printer prepared it with various chemicals and set it up for the printing. This is a very labor-intensive process because each plate must be properly aligned to correctly register the colors. The printer and I began in June 1985 and it took us three months to finish the print. The limited edition of one hundred was printed withmore transparent ink on a fine hand-made paper. The finished work had the appearance of a pastel drawing.

Over the years, I had considered enhancing the Francis of Assisi lithograph, always wondering how much more colorful and elaborate I could make it. At last, in 1998, I turned to the last remaining lithograph and used it to guide me in applying acrylic paints. I worked on each miniature scene to bring out the color and to refine the details. As I embellished it with many more elements and enlarged the borders, it became one of my most complex paintings. Three months later, the *Francis of Assisi* painting was completed, very much changed from the original lithograph.

Francis of Assisi ©1999 acrylic painting by John August Swanson
Image size: 30" x 22 "
www.JohnAugustSwanson.com